Excellence is
Written into
Existence

Excellence is Written into Existence

An Educator's Discovery

MYA HUFF

Excellence is Written in Existence
An Educator's Discovery

© 2021 by Mya Huff

ISBN: 978-0-9906520-6-9

All rights reserved. No part of this book may be reproduced in any form or by any means, electronic or mechanical, including photocopying, recording, or by any information storage and retrieval system, without permission in writing from the publisher.

The following contains accounts of specific events. All names have been changed to protect the identities of all individuals.

To order copies in bulk please contact: *info.MyaHuff@gmail.com*

Published in the United States of America

Contents

Recovery:
Acknowledging it Happened   1
Educators are Pillars   3
Restore Trust   5

Looking into Distance Learning:
The Beginning   11
It Takes Time   14
Less is More   17
Openness and Unity   20
Repairing What is Broken   22

Social Distancing in the Classroom   29

Glimpses of Destiny:
Every Single One   32
Cody's Story   34

A New Approach:
Free Choice   36

Academia:
No Limitations   44
Cultivate Fresh Soil   46
Data Analysis Meeting with Students   48
A Refection of Self   50
The Homework Debacle   51
Inform, So They Know   54
Put it Within Their Reach   56
A Little Compassion   59

Contents

Advocate and Cover:
It Wasn't Good Enough   71
The Fine Print   74

Confidence in Your Craft: 77

Beyond Physical Safety: 82

Fun and Accountability:
Lesson Learned   84
Then Some Days   87

Affirm   89
Scaffold How you Affirm   91

Create a Dialogue:
Ask the Question   97
Open Door Policy   99
Weekly Communication Helps   104

Leadership   106

It Is Written:
A New Name   110

Excellence is Written into Existence

An Educator's Discovery

MYA HUFF

Recovery

Acknowledging it Happened

For there to be recovery, there has to be loss—loss of something or someone. Sometimes we lose things that are replaceable, like a material object or even a job. Sometimes we lose things that are irreplaceable, like people and time. Loss can be that much more detrimental when it happens all at once, and you don't see it coming. Isn't that a mirror image of life this past year? As a nation we lost so much—people, health, financial security and, most of all, peace of mind.

As we enter the new school year, our journey transcends the realms of academics, so there is a new job description for every educator, mentor, coach, and administrator. We have to give our scholars time and space to acknowledge the loss of friends, loved ones, food security, financial security, a nurturing environment, or a safe haven where they can tell someone if something is wrong.

Loss is usually followed by a season of mourning. What that looks like varies from person to person. There are children all over this nation who haven't been given an environment to mourn safely.

In March 2020 we sent students home with packets, tablets, and plenty of schoolwork. But when did we, as a nation, stop to ask how they were doing? So many youths continue to suffer in silent isolation, uncertain of what tomorrow may bring. We silenced them, even though it was not intentional. Their voices often have been drowned out by political issues and social injustices, not that those issues aren't important or didn't have a direct effect on them.

The saving grace is that when there is loss, there is something to be found. As educators it's our job to help our students recapture every good thing they deserve—self-confidence, the freedom to dream, validation, a safe environment, and academic progress. There is life after even the worst storm.

As educators I encourage you this school year to plan for your classroom beyond academia because ignoring students' social and emotional wellbeing this school year would be a grave mistake. Let students laugh, cry, and scream out loud if they need to. This is to be a school year of release. Students deserve a moment to finally lift the weight of the world off their shoulders.

No matter how out of sorts things may become this school year, our young scholars must remain our top priority. Get ready because scholars are going to hit the threshold of your classroom door searching for emotional, mental, and academic stability. There has been a significant loss; students everywhere have a desire to be found.

Educators Are Pillars

After a year of distance learning, one thing educators need is a moment to decompress. Millions around the globe are oblivious to the mental toll distance learning took on many educators—the sleepless nights, time not spent with their own families, and feelings of being overwhelmed. So yes, teachers need a time of recovery as well.

I also encourage educators to identify your own loss or grief. Maybe you lost a family member or your passion for teaching. But you made it, and here you are. Give yourself permission to feel and to grieve. Start the internal process of healing. You are not defeated, and this nation needs you.

Even though some may acknowledge recovery from the past year is needed, I contend that teachers also need to recover from many difficult years before the pandemic, from years of being unheard and unseen, to recover from being underpaid, overworked, and underappreciated. Teachers need to recover from mandates issued by individuals who haven't set foot in a classroom in years. Those individuals demand teachers educate and relate to their students using strategies that are outdated and ineffective.

This nation owes good educators an apology. Educators have been taken for granted and viewed as glorified babysitters. But the reality is that your children's teachers are also counselors, nurses, and voices of reason. Those teachers continue to push forward even when life seems to be too much.

I want educators everywhere to know that you are not forgotten. As challenging as this pandemic has been, America has been reminded that it can't do this without us, the educators. Parents can't go to work, businesses can't operate, and society cannot function. A nation does not advance without effective educators. We prepare the next generation to carry the baton across the finish line. We prepare minds to fan the flame that makes our nation a superpower. Educators are everything, so take a moment to exhale. I would say to every school district: get it right this time. We educators are not an option; we are compulsory. Treat us with the respect we deserve.

Restore Trust

As the world makes an effort to return to a sense of normalcy, we see a hesitancy among some parents to send their children back to the classroom. The reason for that mistrust varies. But trust must be restored everywhere this school year, trust between families and the educational system.

For a second, I would like us to consider the situation from a parent's perspective. For years, millions of parents couldn't depend on their child's school to provide the simple necessities for a first-class education—updated textbooks, well-maintained school buildings, or even a pencil. Ventilation systems were not up to date, which meant students weren't even breathing clean air. Now the government is asking those same parents to send their children back to institutions that haven't properly cared for their needs in years.

Within the last year the curtains were pulled back, the imperfections in the educational sector were exposed, and that unveiling was hideous. It showed how disingenuous, racist, and marginalized pockets of our educational system are. Before the pandemic, students attending school every day was, in some ways, a smoke screen. It gave the perception that all children were being properly educated. It was assumed the same opportunities and resources were extended to all students across the nation, no matter their zip code or socioeconomic class. But if we didn't know it before, we know now that such a view is far from the truth.

We teach our students that receiving a proper education takes more than just showing up. Attendance is major piece of the puzzle, but what are you working on once you arrive? But this issue isn't about students; it's about those in positions of power within the educational sector who have been absent for some time. School districts want students to show up and perform, but those same districts haven't shown up for students in years.

It takes a little more than a town hall meeting or a PTA gathering. It definitely takes more than sitting on a school board. Our educational system has failed both teachers and scholars year after year. Schools are begging for funding to simply provide tissue for restrooms, nutritious lunch programs, and to fill their staffing needs. The only way trust in the educational system is going to be restored is through permanent change.

Parents are not interested in empty promises and political slogans when it comes to the wellbeing of their children. They would prefer to see words put into action. There needs to be evidence of advancement that is consistent and aligned with the best interests of each child. The government, political figures, and school districts want students present and accounted for, but those entities have to show up too. Our government's truancy record when it comes to making sure all children receive a first-class education is horrible.

Students, teachers, and families will return to school buildings this fall. When teachers take attendance, we hope they will find that the changes so desperately needed to provide an equal and excellent education for our children present as well.

Recovery

Visualize | Script | Plan

Excellence is Written into Existence

~Example: Strategies for Student Recovery~

☐ Below are examples of activities you may implement during the process of student recovery this school year.

Social	Emotional	Academics	Mental Health
-Daily ice breakers is a great place to start. It requires students to communicate with others within their peer group they otherwise may not. -Focus on building relationships -Research social skills activities and games for youth.	-Help students identify what they are feeling. A great tool is activities that promote self-expression. -Artwork: Drawing, Painting -Using Words: Writing a poem, song, or story. -Teach students to manage their feelings after they have identified what they are.	-Data Collection Having students take a diagnostic by subject is a great start (math, Ela/reading, science) -Lesson plans for the first two months of school should include reviewing critical standards from the previous grade.	-Activities that promote mental health -Teach students to practice deep breathing. -Movement breaks -DEAR Time: Reading relaxes the body and calms the mind

Excellence is Written into Existence

~Strategies for Student Recovery~

- Please use the following chart to plan what student recovery will look like in your classroom. Keep your organization's objectives and personal teaching style in mind.

Social	Emotional	Academics	Mental Health

Excellence is Written into Existence

∽Looking Into∽ Distance Learning

The Beginning

It was a Friday in March 2020. The atmosphere in the building was one of urgency. There had been whispers all week about school closings taking place across the nation, state by state, district by district. For that entire week it felt like we were just waiting our turn. When we entered the building that fateful Friday, we were greeted with the news that, for at least the next few weeks, there would be a brief intermission in face-to-face learning. Students were to learn online instead.

I quickly made copies of packets, login badges, and anything else I could think of to help students learn over the next three weeks. Then the school started handing out technology to one student after another. I walked back and forth in the classroom, physically packing my scholars' things. It felt like I was sending them away, and I needed to make sure they had everything they needed.

But my students could already sense that feeling of separation. One by one they started asking questions:

"Ms. Huff, where are we going?"

"Ms. Huff, why are you packing so much stuff in our bookbags?"

"Ms. Huff, when are we coming back?"

I told my children with confidence and certainty, "It's only for three weeks." Their faces reflected excitement mixed with concern. But no one knew that Friday in March would be the last time I would see my scholars in 2020.

In the weeks that followed, the only interactions I had with my scholars were online or on the phone. Some calls were from students needing help with their schoolwork. Other calls were from parents venting their frustrations. Some calls were from tearful scholars unable to cope with how life had changed so fast and how the pandemic was setting in.

Then there were those scholars who were literally stuck. As a nation, we were reminded that, for millions of children, school is an escape; it's the daily avenue to some type of relief. When my scholars would call and ask when they could come back to school, was this pandemic almost over, I couldn't give them a definitive answer. I had already given them my word once, and due to circumstances beyond anyone's control, that promise had been broken. Those three weeks had come and gone.

There were teachers everywhere who felt that same sense of helplessness, the one where you knew a student needed you, but there was nothing you could do. Students needed their teachers to remind them they were rock stars, that the world was at their feet, that they could do absolutely anything. Some teachers saw firsthand that their students needed someone to simply be kind to them. But the teachers couldn't rescue their students; the teachers could no longer be that someone.

Make no mistake: there are little ones all over this nation who need someone to rescue them from the environment they were subject to during quarantine. But all teachers could do most days was try to lift our students' spirits and ask them to please hold on a little longer. We were the reminder that they could make it.

Then you began to hear the stories of teachers who were going above and beyond for their scholars. Many had been doing so in their classrooms every day long before the world shut down. But thanks to the pandemic, the world was seeing caring teachers firsthand. The lengths educators worldwide were willing to go to just to make sure their scholars' heads stayed above water were magnificent and selfless. Teachers were driving to students' homes to drop off schoolwork and technology. Teachers were delivering food to children who otherwise might have gone hungry. Sometimes a teacher would drive an hour or more simply to drop off a pack of pencils. Educators were building digital platforms from scratch and spending time and their own money to purchase and then learn new software. All the while there were those in this nation who still had the audacity to utter the words, "You aren't doing enough." But it was only the beginning. It was only March 2020.

It Takes Time

Something I observed during distance learning was some parents' swift and, at times, overbearing response to their children's educational process. I can't tell you the number of times students would answer a question and, if they got it wrong, the parents' first response was, "Why don't you know that?" And that response was often delivered in a tone that was demeaning rather than encouraging. Education is a process, but most of the time parents only see the results (progress reports, report cards, promotions). But there is a big in between. Trial and error are a normal facet of daily life in the classroom.

I tell my students all the time that I don't care if they don't get an answer right every time, but I do care if they try. If they fall, that's OK because, as an educator, I'm there to pick them up. But scolding a child over a wrong answer creates a punitive environment, one that too many children existed in for months during quarantine. Parents, in one breath, would complain that they weren't trained to be teachers, but with the next breath, they wouldn't let teachers help them. Oh, the irony.

During distance learning I explained to some parents that there would be days when the students would be covering a new standard. In other words, be patient. Achieving mastery is not the absence of mistakes or misconceptions. Those potholes are what make the journey beautiful and the student's triumph that much sweeter.

What I also noticed was that some parents had the mindset that home schooling was a competition. Their child needed to outperform every other scholar on the Zoom call. Then there were those parents whose main concern was how they looked if their child got an answer wrong. Such parents were unrealistic and narcissistic. I explained to some parents that they were making distance learning much harder for their children than it needed to be. The children already felt embarrassed about being wrong in front of their peers. On top of that, their entire class could hear the parent in the background yelling about the wrong answer.

The last thing I wanted to see was a scholar completely shut down because of negative responses they might receive from their own parents if they gave a wrong answer.

For some of my students whose parents wouldn't let up, I started putting the lesson questions in the chat. For example, if I was on question five I would write a direct message to the students like this: "What is your response to question seven?" That way, the scholars knew what question was coming, and they could respond in the chat before doing so verbally. If they got it right, I would then ask the question aloud. If the answer was wrong in the chat, I would scaffold or reword the question until they could work out their reasoning.

If the student only answered one part of the question correctly, I would split the question into two parts so the scholar could answer the part they got right, then I would present the second part of the question to another scholar. That process was an effort to keep building their confidence.

Sounds like a lot, right? Well, some parents were a lot and, frankly, they were overbearing. Education is a journey that should be enjoyable—one day, one standard, one task, one victory at a time. Eventually, all those small victories manifest themselves into a beautiful canvas of students' hard work and determination to win.

Less Is More

During distance learning one thing students had to build was stamina. Many would agree that a child staring at a screen from 8:30 in the morning until 4:15 in the afternoon isn't a healthy situation. When the last school year started, the organization I worked for set a schedule calling for core subjects to be covered throughout the day: math, for instance, would start at 9 a.m., but reading wouldn't start until 2 p.m.

A pattern I saw was that students were present and accounted for in the morning, but by the afternoon, numbers sometimes dropped. Students might return eventually, but when they did it was often an hour into the lesson. As a solution, I changed my students' schedule so that all core subjects were in the morning (8:30 a.m. to 12:30 p.m.). Then we would break for lunch and recess. That left small group and time on instructional websites for the afternoon.

The new schedule ensured a few key points. First, I was confident 95 percent of my class would receive both the reading and math lessons every day. It also gave students a bit of relief and encouragement to log back in during the afternoon. Small groups always included fun activities at the end, and students genuinely loved working on online instructional websites.

Another tweak I made during the first month of school was that I released my students every day between 1:15 and 1:30 p.m. We had to build up to being online from 8:30 a.m. to 4:15 p.m. Students had been out of school since March of

2020, so coming back in the fall with a demand to stare at a screen for six hours was a big ask.

To be fair, the first month of school was all review from the previous grade, so there was some flexibility. But it worked. My class had one of the best attendance records in the entire organization during distance learning. Attendance included three aspects: showing up, staying logged in and engaged, and returning after lunch break. When present in the school the building students often take the first week to learn routines and procedures. In the same way last fall students needed a second to become acclimated to the new normal and mental demands of distance learning.

Openness and Unity

As we know, distance learning has required patience and adjustments. How do you build a classroom culture online? It starts with the little things. For example, I can't tell you how many mornings my students and I made breakfast together. Literally everyone took their laptop or tablet to the kitchen and prepared something to eat. For some students it was a bowl of cereal, for others a breakfast pastry, and for others a granola bar. But that activity meant something to my children. We weren't talking about academics or reviewing work. Sometimes it was like having ten cooking channels going at once because they wanted to show their classmates and me what they were making and how they were making it.

Another big hit was Show and Tell, but my students called it Look and See. They wanted to show what they had bought at the store over the weekend. Students wanted to show what they received for Christmas, their pets, or how they decorated their new room. It was their way of opening up and welcoming their classmates into their world. It was an icebreaker that extended the entire school year. It helped the students learn about each other's likes and dislikes.

Another thing that happened in my classroom every Friday afternoon was the showing of a children's movie. Oh yes. Students looked forward to it all week. They could watch a movie with their classmates and have a snack. The movie was always of their choosing—as long as it was age appropriate. Again, we were still separated, but that was something we could do together.

Another thing we did was play video games together online. The digital play store was a lifesaver.

Some of the best morning meetings were when families started to chime in over impromptu subjects. One day a student was making ramen noodles for breakfast, so his classmate asked what he put in them. Then all the students started chiming in, and their parents began to show up on camera. Everyone started discussing what brand of ramen noodles they purchased and their favorite recipes. That was one of the liveliest morning meetings we had all year. Moms, dads, grandparents, aunts, and uncles wanted to add to the conversation about ramen noodles. But the big takeaway was the building of a community. Parents who had never spoken with one another introduced themselves.

Be creative as an educator. Everything shouldn't be about schoolwork every second of every day. Take time to ask your students how they're doing and if they want to share anything with their peers. Little things make a big difference.

Repairing What is Broken

Parents taking on the role of educators this past year, in some ways, has fractured parent-child relationships. Parents felt pressure to make sure their children didn't fall behind academically, and children felt pressure from parents who were pushing too hard. As educators, we can help fix that.

So what is one method for repairing those parent-child relationships this school year? Start by sharing some good news. A great conversation starter for family members is a child's accomplishments in school. It could be a social or emotional milestone or an academic accomplishment. Tailor the good news for each student. This year, make it a point to share positive milestones with parents in your classroom. We could all stand to hear some good news on a consistent basis.

As a teacher, you won't be able to do that every day for every child in your class. But set a goal that each child will have an individualized, positive message sent home. If you don't have anything positive to share about academics, then share a leadership role the scholar took on, tell about something nice the scholar did for someone, or offer evidence of some other success.

That strategy may help parents be less defensive on days when you may not have great news because, well, scholars make mistakes. You never want parents to feel like they only hear from you when something is wrong.

Good news will give parents a chance to experience a sigh of relief. It also creates an avenue for parents to say to their scholar, "I'm proud of you." And those few words mean everything to a child. Every child wants the approval or validation of their parents. Some scholars never heard those words during quarantine, not because they weren't trying their best, but because mom or dad trying to play the role of educator and parent may have been too much. So let the healing begin, and let it start with us.

Good News

Excellence is Written into Existence

~Example: Good News Tracker~

☐ This tracker is a way for you to make sure each child has a personalized message shared with parents weekly. You can check off what type of growth you shared for each student. In a perfect world each student would receive two checks a week. This is for your records only.

Student Name	Academic Glow	Social/Emotional Glow	Leadership Role/Classroom Jobs	Class Glow
1. Jasmin		✓		✓
2. Trevor			✓	✓
3. Chase	✓			✓
4. Kiana	✓			✓
5. Dana			✓	✓

Excellence is Written into Existence

~Good News Tracker~

☐ Create your own communication tracker for your classroom. Incorporate specific areas you would like to highlight for your scholars.

Student Name	(Category)	(Category)	(Category)	(Category)
1.				
2.				
3.				
4.				
6.				
7.				

Excellence is Written into Existence

~Example: Class Leadership Roles~

☐ The following are examples of leadership roles or responsibilities you may share with parents. Its helps if responsibilities are rotated daily or weekly. Most teachers have a chart hanging in the classroom where they simply switch out names. Take a photo of the chart and post it for parents viewing.

Classroom Jobs

Job Title	Scholars' Name
Pencil Personnel	John
Lunch Transitision	Danelle
Paper Committee	Jordan

**Share with parents what their scholar's role may entail.

Student Government Roles
(May be rotated monthly)

Office Held	Scholars' Name
Class Secretary	Brian
Communications Director	Stacey
Class Senator	Natalie

**Share with parents what their scholar's role may entail.

Excellence is Written into Existence

~Class Leadership Roles~

☐ Create a leadership chart for your classroom. Be creative with titles for example, the title pencil personnel is another way to say pencil sharpener. They are responsible for making sure there are enough pencils sharpened and distributed before lessons begin. They may also sharpen pencils at the end of the day. Plan your own system. Create your own categories.

Job Title	*Scholars' Name*	*Job Title*	*Scholars' Name*
(Job Category)		(Job Category)	

Excellence is Written into Existence

Social Distancing in the Classroom

Fast forward to March of 2021 when schools were taking the leap to reopen, most using a hybrid model. Anxieties for teachers, students, and their families were high. There were many guidelines to help ensure the safety of everyone. The big day finally arrived, and what we all knew, despite the narrative from the media, finally manifested itself in real time: social distancing in the classroom was mostly a myth, although it sounded nice.

Now I want to give some context. When it came to my students' seat placements in the classroom, they were socially distanced. But let's talk about the reality of them staying in their seats the entire day. That was never going to happen. First, you have the fact that students had been home for a year, moving about as they pleased. When they wanted to go to the kitchen or sit in another room in the house, they did. Once students were back in school, it was clear that people who don't deal with children created the guidelines that said students should sit for hours at a time. Unrealistic.

When we returned to the classroom, those guidelines lasted all of four days. My students hadn't seen each other for over a year, and human interaction was something they craved. Did they all have their own supplies? Yes, and they did well in not touching other students' materials and manipulatives.

It was keeping them out of each other's personal bubbles that was the trick.

Reading all those guidelines spelled "fear" to me. Honestly, I didn't want that type of environment for my children. If I had enforced every single guideline, it would have created an atmosphere that neither my students nor I would have wanted. My strict button with my students was pressed when it came to safety measures such as was wearing their masks and washing their hands. Did they work in groups and with partners? Yes, they did, and they kept coming back to my desk with no regard for my personal space even though I kept saying, "Don't come up here." I said it with a smile, but I was serious. I told them, "I can hear you from your seat."

The routine was that they would raise their hand, I would ask what they needed, and they would walk up to my desk. I would gaze in disbelief and say, "You back up here?" They thought it was the funniest thing. But my kids were happy. No child in my classroom got sick, and they weren't miserable.

Am I saying to run your classroom that way? No. But try your best to create an environment that doesn't make students frantic or that promotes anxiety and fear. Negative feelings, research shows, can affect a person's mental state and bodily functions. If you say, "Don't touch this . . . You're too close to your classmate . . . You can't play over there . . . You can't sit here . . . Don't breathe too many times" all day every day, you can see what a negative atmosphere that would create. Of course, I'm kidding with that last one, but you get the point.

I needed my children to know they were safe. The world, in some ways, may have been in chaos, but when my students hit the threshold of my classroom door, calm and peace greeted them. I needed their parents to be confident that I would do everything in my power to not only make sure their children remained safe and healthy but that they would enjoy being back in the classroom.

We did so well after the first few weeks that I started getting messages from parents who had initially opted out of in-person learning that said their child was asking to come back to the school building. Students watched from home all day, and some desperately wanted to be in the classroom. Parents wanted to know if it was too late for their child to attend in person. But they also were transparent in saying they were still worried. So as the weeks went on, our numbers grew. Students were only supposed to come to class twice a week based on their grouping, but most started coming every single day. The administration approved it, and I was more than happy to have my students back.

So when you return to the classroom this year, do so with a firm grip on reality. If you're calm, your students will be calm. But if you're on edge all day, that will become the culture in your classroom. That is not a way of life that is conducive for a child's development. We can't get back to normalcy if we don't start doing things that are normal. Students wanting to collaborate academically or to simply interact with their friends is normal. Social distancing in the classroom, that's cute, but I need my students to be children without a care in the world. Guidelines need to have a foundation of confidence for students and their families.

Glimpses of Destiny

Every Single One

As educators it's our job to motivate and develop children. We need to challenge the scholar who's performing at the top of the class while also developing our scholars who are on or below grade level. As an educator it's your challenge to make every child in your class a superstar—yes, every single one. Every child is not going to achieve a 4.0, and every child may not be in the top social tier. But all students deserve your best effort to help them reach as high as they can.

The first step is recognizing each student's gifts, talents, and interests. I had one student I'll call John who received services. When the school year started, he was so timid that he didn't want to speak up in class or interact socially. But I noticed John was always drawing. Even during class, he would sketch throughout the lesson. He was extremely talented and would have put many adults who attended art school to shame.

So I sat John down one day to have a conversation about the appropriate times to draw in class. But during that conversation I also handed him a sketch book I had purchased, the kind professionals use. Then I told John he was now in charge of decorating the class bulletin board, and once a month he would choose a team of his peers to help him. He stared at me in shock. The last thing I told him was to make a list of decorations he needed for the October bulletin board, which would be his first time leading.

I took the school credit card for our grade and bought John everything he asked for. He and three other students decorated that bulletin board. Every month the school had a competition for the best bulletin board. Top prize was a pizza party and a trophy that was kept in the winning classroom for the month. In October, we won! Guess whose desk that trophy sat on? The same kid who wouldn't speak because of a lack of confidence. John had become the young man who was now leading a different group of his peers every month. That experience opened other opportunities for him socially. Now John is shining bright by simply using his gift.

But I planted the seed that created the opportunity. I didn't just tell him, "Stop drawing." No, I had a kid who was coming along academically by working at it daily. But I wanted him to know he was more than just a GPA. And so, with John leading the way, we won the bulletin board competition three times that school year.

As educators, if we see our scholars every day and only offer them lessons and academic tasks, we have not done our job. My job as an educator is to teach my scholars to imagine and to dream. My message to my scholars is that academic success is the icing on the cake because they are so much more than a test score.

Cody's Story

At the beginning of the school year students were given the task of writing what they wanted to be when they grew up and explaining why. There was a young man we'll call Cody who wrote that he wanted to be a comedian. His reasoning was that he liked to see people smile. Here's the kicker: at the age of eight, Cody's' comedic timing was brilliant. He was not a class clown, nor did he cause disruptions. But at least twice a day he would say something that would have his peers, other staff, and me shedding tears of laughter. He genuinely had a gift.

One day I sat Cody down and asked, "What motivates your sense of humor?"

"At home, when I tell jokes," he said, "everyone is not so sad."

Cody's family was living in a shelter, and neither he nor his siblings had food security. Some may say he learned to make others laugh so he could keep from crying.

During that same conversation I told Cody that during every Fun Friday he would have a five- minute set if he wanted it.

"What's a set?" he asked.

So I showed him clips of clean comedy where comedians were sharing their craft with thousands of people all over the world. Cody's eyes lit up as he watched. He saw people who looked like him earn a living by walking in their own destiny.

The first two Fridays Cody stood up in front of his peers, he told two jokes and sat down. He was nervous, but he did well. Going into the third week I encouraged Cody to use his everyday experiences as material. I suggested he tell a joke about football practice or shopping at Walmart with his mom. The next week he got up and did the full five minutes. Not every joke resonated with me as an adult, but he connected with the audience of his peers in a language they understood, and that was the goal. For the rest of the school year, Cody's' friends were attentive whenever he stood to speak.

What's the purpose of telling Cody's story? Give your students space to walk in their gifts and sow seeds in them early that promote confidence. My hope is that, by standing in front of twenty-one of his peers and telling jokes, someday Cody will stand before full stadiums to share his story and his gift with the world. It's not always what you do and say as an educator. Your actions also need to carry the message that you believe in your students and their dreams and that you are confident they can make those dreams come true. All they have to do is walk in their destiny. Cody was doing something comedians do every day. He was giving his audience, some of whom were in the same economic situation he was, a reason to smile.

~A New Approach~

Free Choice

One of the vital approaches I promote in my classroom is free choice because it is directly connected to critical thinking and reasoning skills. This practice not only ties into academics but social skills as well. I see free choice being promoted at certain educational institutions, but not so much in the inner city.

How are students supposed to build the confidence to tackle a challenging task if, as an educator, you're telling them what to do every second of the day? The only thing the scholars decide is how many breaths they take. That may sound extreme, but it's a common reality.

Overbearing is what you call that. The teacher tells the students where to sit, how to sit, where to stand in line, how to stand in line, who they can sit next to at lunch, even what games they can play during recess. That type of atmosphere is far more appropriate for a juvenile detention center than a school. Contrary to popular belief, students don't need to be controlled in order to evolve and grow as individuals and scholars. Free choice does not mean that a teacher is completely hands off in any situation. Free choice is also not the absence of expectations. But let students figure some things out on their own.

I will use math as an example. Some students completely shut down when they see a word problem; they want no part of it. That attitude goes a little deeper than a scholar seeing the problem as a challenge. For some students, a switch clicks in their mind, and they think, "I have a problem, and no one is here to tell me exactly how to solve it." As an educator you want them to turn on the power of reasoning. But when have they exercised that power any other time throughout the school day?

The proper response for a student who gets stuck on a math problem or who is faced with any challenge is this: *I have a problem I don't completely understand. But I can identify what stands out to me and start from there.*

Most young people are being programmed in school by being told what to think and how they should perceive the world around them. There is only a small segment of youth that is being taught how to think, problem solve, and use the power of reasoning. Most youth never tap into that part of their mind because the invitation to exercise free thinking has never been extended. Brilliance comes from the freedom to push the limits and step outside the boundaries of what society deems normal.

If you give children blocks of clay, they will mold a sculpture that is unique to their own thinking. But in education, too often we hand children a sculpture that has already been molded, which blocks each student's individual creative power. Instead, we should set students' intellectual, social, and emotional abilities free and watch them bloom.

Students are capable of much more than many people think they are.

I would encourage every educator to introduce the concept of free choice into your classroom culture. Start with simple tasks. You can do so gradually. It may not exist in every facet of the day, but there is still a place for it. Inform your students of the purpose of having free choice. It's not to do as they please but to make informed, logical, and helpful decisions through the avenues of critical thinking and the power of reasoning.

❑ **Small ways to implement free choice**

Free Choice: Example 1

Most classrooms have the rule, "Raise your hand before you get out of your seat." This is where building a culture by promoting free choice and encouraging reasoning comes into play. As a class we have a conversation. I use the example of college. I ask my students, "If you're sitting in a college classroom and your professor is lecturing, are you going to get up to get you favorite glitter pencil out of you bookbag?" My students respond, "No." So then I ask, "Well, when is a good time to get up?" The correct answer: when the lecture is done. Now full transparency: this is not something my students master within the first month of school. But by mid-October, they usually have it down.

Movement: A Visual for Students	
Free Choice	**Power of Reasoning**
❑ I am allowed to move around the classroom freely.	❑ Is this the best time to get out of my seat? ❑ Will it cause a distraction?

Free Choice: Example 2

Another window of the day where you may implement free choice is DEAR time. (Drop Everything and Read) Some students are always told what book or text to read. But then there is the power of free choice. For example, if, as a class, we are reading informational text for the second quarter, I tell my students to pick a topic of their choosing. Some students want to read about polar bears; other students want to learn about volcanoes. Let them have a say.

DEAR Time: A Visual for Students	
Free Choice	**Power of Reasoning**
☐ I am allowed pick any topic of my choosing.	☐ Does the title I chose *inform* me about this topic? ☐ Does it have the certain text features? ☐ Can I identify at least one of the five informational text structures within the text?

Another aspect of DEAR time is where students choose to read. In some classrooms, students are required to sit up straight with their back at a perfect 90-degree angle while reading independently. But why not let them pick a spot in the room that is comfortable for them? I worked at one organization, where student population had top reading scores in the city. During DEAR time, you had students lying under their desk, some sitting in a corner, on the carpet, some students sat on top of their desk, and others wanted to be in the library portion of the classroom. But for that 30-minute window, you could hear a pin drop. What is the point? Even with the freedom to choose where they sat, students knew the expectation. It was an enjoyable experience, not another dictated portion of their day.

DEA R Time: A Visual for Students	
Free Choice	**Power of Reasoning**
☐ I am allowed sit anywhere I would like during DEAR time	☐ If I sit by myself, I am more likely to remain focused ☐ If I sit in an area close to my best friend in class, I am more likely to become distracted

Free Choice: Example 3

Another example of free choice is when students eat. My students are welcome to eat whenever they choose. We are in the school building from 7:45 a.m. until 4:15 p.m. It would be irresponsible of me as an adult to tell children they are only allowed to eat once, and they only have thirty minutes to do so. My expectation is for them to clean up after themselves and be cognizant about the time of day when it comes to their food choices.

Snacks: A Visual for Students	
Free Choice	**Power of Reasoning**
☐ I am allowed to eat when I choose	☐ Should I be eating potato chips at 9:30am? ☐ What is a better food choice to start my day?

That's something they can figure out on their own, but that doesn't mean we didn't have to review that kind of reasoning as a class. But after a while, using their freedom appropriately becomes the norm. Students now understand, we eat a breakfast that fuels our brain for the day and promotes a balanced eating regimen. If families are aware of our classroom culture, they will buy into it too. And it works. My students' families often use their freedom creatively and bring snacks like seaweed sheets, aloe drinks, and bags of grapes. Set the expectation, let students take it from there.

Academia

No Limitations

As an educator, two things I'm not interested in regarding students' academic performance are perfection and excuses. My expectations are high and, in my experience, students almost always rise to meet them. I have seen people in the educational system publicly proclaim the education a child is provided shouldn't depend on zip codes, but then they set expectations based on zip codes. Sometimes there are preconceived notions of what scholars are capable of that will seep into an educator's content planning.

Perfection is replaced with growth in my classroom. For students at the top of the class, my focus is on their continued progress. If you are what I call a "bubble kid," how have you grown? Even my scholars who receive services are expected to show growth. Contrary to popular belief in the educational community, "perfection" is not the only thing that deserves honor.

People have asked me why I push my students so hard? The answer is simple. It's because I know, without a doubt, that no one is setting a low bar for their counterparts. Transparency with students and their families is what I offer from day one. I am going to push my students to the limit and, sometimes, beyond what they believe is possible. For that I make no apologies. My approach has unlocked potential and revealed gifts in my students they didn't even know were there.

For years students have entered my classroom the first week of school and said things like, "I'm just not good at math." My question to them is always, "Who told you that?" Parents have come for parent-teacher conferences and, before I say one word, they begin the conversation with, "Ms. Huff, I just want you to know she has always struggled in math," or "Math is just not his strong subject." Then parents' faces are puzzled when I sometimes respond with, "That can't be true; your child is one of the top performers in the class."

Parents sometimes come in on the defensive with the perspective that their child has limitations when, in fact, the only limitation is the child's mindset. A scholar walking in and telling me what they're not capable of is a defeatist attitude. I let my scholars know that as long as their brain is on, there is more to achieve. If today wasn't perfect, so what? Tomorrow is a new day, and they have another chance.

Cultivate Fresh Soil

As an educator you need to ensure that your classroom is a place where *all* children excel and where excellence is not optional. If you plant a rose in concrete, it will wither and die. It's not that the rose didn't have the potential to bloom and become vibrant, but it has to be planted in the right soil. Likewise, for students to bloom, rigor must be mixed into the soil. Rigor can sometimes be intimidating to students, but it shouldn't be. Rigor is simply another avenue for students to obtain mastery and experience winning.

Cultivating is simply turning over and breaking up the soil. This school year, cultivate the soil in your classroom. When a farmer tills the land, he is removing whatever could be harmful when it's harvest time. This school year, break up old mindsets and pull the weeds of complacency where doing the bare minimum is enough.

Cultivating the soil also involves digging. How deep farmers dig depends on what they intend to plant. For example, planting a vegetable garden has a recommended depth of six to ten inches. But for potatoes, the recommended depth is eighteen inches. What harvest are you trying to manifest in your students? Is it work ethic, perseverance, or simply the willingness to try?

Cultivating also raises a question for us as educators: how deep are we willing to dig within ourselves? Are we complacent and willing to accept a garden that looks good but that has been planted so shallow that the seeds will never take root? Those withering plants are sometimes our practices or classroom management styles that need fine tuning. Or are you looking to manifest a harvest that takes time to nurture but that will be sustainable?

We have already discussed how free choice is tied into academics. I inform my students they will be successful, but how their journey unfolds is dependent on them. Failure is not an option. Excellence is not a rule; it's a way of life.

But that system is built on a powerful foundation of these three fundamentals:

1. Accountability.
2. Breaking the mindset of defeat.
3. Building a space where mistakes are merely steps toward mastery.

Data Analysis Meetings with Students

Data analysis is not only for educators, it's particularly useful for students as well, so we have data analysis meetings in the classroom, and students quickly become deeply invested. So what do such meetings entail? First, I try to establish a corporate feel. Fresh water bottles are placed on the students' desks, they take out notepads that are exclusively for the data meetings, and they are given fancy pens. It's never too early to learn good business practices or boardroom etiquette. Throughout the year we learn common expressions used in business meetings, which helps students better articulate their thoughts.

But back to the data analysis meeting. First, we review the notes from the last meeting and what goals we set. Second, we go over the agenda or the objective for the current meeting. Next, we dive into our data from a quiz, exit ticket, or an exam and review our class average. Then we review individual scores. Of course, that is done in "presentation mode" so students' names are replaced with aliases like Speed Racer. As a result, students see an anonymous visual breakdown of their peers' performances. The purpose is to help the students recognize trends for themselves.

Identifying trends is a skill I teach from the beginning of the school year. It can be as simple as students saying, "Ms. Huff, a lot of people got number five on the exam wrong" or "Ms. Huff, everyone in the class got number two right." We then review the correct answers. The last part of our data meeting is devoted to identifying the standards we mastered and those we may need to review. All the data is visual and shown at the click of a button. Our meetings usually last no more than fifteen minutes. Time should be allotted for students to ask questions and voice any questions, concerns, or ideas they may have.

The next day we continue our data analysis in small groups that go into a deeper evaluation of the standards. Contrary to popular belief, small groups should be interchangeable daily, not weekly or monthly. You will have one or two groups that are constant, meaning you will see certain students daily, regardless. Other than that, small groups should be fluid.

Data analysis also can be a quick check in literally two minutes. For example, my students will ask how they did as a class on an exit ticket. I'll say, "We scored a class average of 85 percent," and the students use that information to celebrate or push each other to aim higher. Providing students with visual data of their progress is another aspect of accountability and motivation.

A Reflection of Self

Here is the kicker: before I stand in front of my students to review our performance, I review my own. I take note of what we mastered, but then I go back to the drawing board to review my strategies for those standards where we did not perform well. When you deliver news to your students that more work is needed, you should present a plan for improvement. There is no use in announcing, "Houston, we have a problem," unless you also offer a solution. When my students fall short, the first person I look at is me. What can I do better? How can I scaffold or execute this strategy more effectively?

As an educator you must take responsibility when students fall short and give them all the accolades when they triumph. Of course, you had everything to do with their growth and mastery. But when we come together as a class to celebrate, I tell my students, "This moment is for you." Believe it or not, students will come back and say, "Thank you for teaching us."

Finally, when you have to deliver the hard messages—students need to take more ownership in the test preparation or daily work ethic—be sure to leave them feeling empowered. Never end on a negative note because there is always light at the end of the tunnel, but sometimes students won't see that light unless they believe you see it too.

The Homework Debacle

One year I was working for a particular organization that had a huge problem convincing scholars to do their homework. It was a schoolwide issue. The administration made a major announcement one month into the school year saying that students should no longer be penalized in any way for not doing their homework. That meant teachers couldn't put a zero in the grade book for homework being incomplete. And no other punitive action could be taken either, such as taking away recess. Of course, what was supposed to be a thirty-minute meeting turned into a two-hour dialogue between staff and administration.

The reason the administration gave for the new policy was that parents were complaining they didn't always have time to help their children with their homework. I understand their point, but for me, a better solution would have been instructing teachers not to assign more than thirty minutes of homework a night.

The complaint did not come from the majority but from an exceedingly small number of vocal parents, and the administration's response spoke to the culture of the school. The voice of a few parents had been allowed to dictate what all scholars' academic expectations—or lack thereof—should be. The voice of the few outweighed the long-term academic well-being of the many.

The administration went as far as trying to convince educators, some twenty-year veterans of the classroom, that homework was not a critical component in a child's academic success. I had worked for other schools where, if children did not have homework for even one night, parents wanted to know why, so you see the contrast.

Finally, the administration came up with the idea to take the homework category out of the digital grade book altogether so there was no place to record that data. A few teachers agreed with that decision, but the majority were puzzled and at a loss for words.

Until then, the rule in my classroom was always, "No homework, no recess." My students knew the only exception was if a parent contacted me to let me know a scholar might not have their homework on a particular day, but that wasn't allowed to become a weekly thing.

So I tried the new approach the administration had mandated and announced it to families. After a week, one day right before recess, I lined up all my students who hadn't completed homework in three days, and we went to see my supervisor. I taught multiple sections of the same grade level, so over thirty students stood in that line, and there were only forty-two students in that grade level. My supervisor stepped into the hallway, and I whispered to her who this group was. She gave me the green light and said to go back to what I was doing before.

A few months later, state testing rolled around. Guess whose scholars outperformed their peers by 90 percent or more on a national level? Mine. On the other hand, a slew of "improvement plans" came down for multiple teachers, some of whom had advocated to remove homework from the grade book simply because they didn't want to wrestle with students and certain families about getting it done. So what's the message? Don't take shortcuts.

Beyond teachers' performances being critiqued, the more pressing issue was the students who were not progressing. Those results were a testament to a policy based on laziness on everybody's part. The administration didn't want to anger parents, parents didn't want to be responsible for checking homework, teachers didn't want to battle with students about getting it done, and if students didn't *have* to do homework anymore, they weren't going to do it.

The messaging and results of that one decision set students back and undermined the pursuit of excellence. Especially with those scholars who were already performing below grade level and needed extra practice. In some ways, it was setting scholars up for a rude awakening in the future. During high school or college, no instructor would tell these same students they simply don't have to do homework. Most of all, that decision depleted a level of accountability. Homework is a critical component of mastery. Don't let anyone tell you differently.

Inform, So They Know

When it comes to homework, I am not ashamed to say I will staple one or two extra math problems to the back of a student's regular homework. At the beginning of the school year, students are not happy about that at all. But there is a purpose. Fast forward two months when we're covering a strategy the students really like or when they're struggling through a lesson. Guess what question pops up? "Ms. Huff, can you make an extra problem for me to take home?" That shows me a few things. They are invested in their own success and unafraid to ask for help. It also shows me they have grown accustomed to doing more than what is required. Most likely, the homework that will be assigned will cover whatever standard we tackled that day. But the students are open to more.

Here's the thing: my students know I'm willing to help and that extra resources are available. Sometimes students don't ask questions because they aren't aware of what is available to them. Other times they don't ask because they know they have a teacher who does the bare minimum. God forbid they should ask for anything that would even remotely inconvenience the teacher.

It's the small things. For example, one of the most common excuses students would give me for why they didn't complete their homework was that they lost it. But there is a solution to that tired excuse. I knew most of my children attended aftercare, so they were still in the building after school. So outside my classroom I hung an organizer that had labels for each day of the week. At the end of every day

I put a few extra copies of the homework for that night into the organizer, just in case. If students lost their homework in aftercare, all they had to do was come get another one. Even if students didn't attend aftercare and came in the next morning with the excuse that they had lost their homework, those extra copies were still available. Students also know they can find me at the kidney table every morning, usually reviewing a word problem students struggled with the night before. So if they have questions, they can ask. They usually have thirty to forty-five minutes between the time they arrive and when class starts. The point is, they have every opportunity to turn something into me, so there are no valid excuses.

What do you students know? Is it that you are available for tutoring thirty minutes after school? Is it that you post math notes every day digitally, so families have access in the evenings? Sometimes it's not that students don't want extra help or supplemental resources, it's that they were never informed those options were available. Create an environment where excuses have no place and where more than enough will always be provided.

Put it Within Their Reach

As a society we are programmed to take notice of the best—the best GPA, the fastest person on the field, or the most popular person in the room. As educators we have to recognize that academic success varies. A message I tell my students daily is this: "I don't need you to be like anyone else; I just need your best." One scholar's best may be 3.8, and another's may be 2.7, but that's OK.

Academics don't come easy to every child, and neither does motivation. But, as a society, we only honor those who have the "right outcome," meaning only the children with a certain GPA are recognized for example at the honor roll ceremony. But there are children in that school who worked just as hard, if not harder, for their 2.7 GPA as those with a 3.8 did. In all my years in the education sector, not once have I seen an awards ceremony where students who receive services are recognized. That doesn't sit well with me.

I'll never forget one year when I had four ELL learners in my classroom. One day the school held a huge honor roll celebration for students, but none of those ELL students received invitations. Here's the thing: those ELL students were phenomenal at math but still coming along in reading as anyone would be if they were still learning the English language. It wasn't that those students didn't try. They worked hard daily, so I planned a small celebration in my classroom to recognize their areas of growth.

That is where our jobs as educators come into play. You know your scholars better than the school district or the administrators do, so create moments and opportunities of celebration. I will share one of the ways I roll this out in my classroom.

Like most schools my students take the state testing three times a year. This particular year I was new to the school. It was my first time seeing that testing environment, so as I watched my students test over a span of two days in September. I noticed not one scholar pulled out any scratch paper, which left me dumbfounded, especially when they were taking the math section. I also noticed some scholars finished a section that had more than forty questions in less than thirty minutes. I definitely made a note to myself: we need to dive into test-taking skills.

So when the Christmas season rolled around and it was time to take the second round of the state testing. I informed my scholars there would be rewards. There was excitement in their eyes because they knew when it came to incentives, we always did it big, and everyone had a chance to earn something. There were prizes for students who achieved the top scores, of course, but I added more categories: Best Scratch Paper, Any Amount of Growth, Meeting their Winter Goal, Meeting their Spring Goal early, and Taking Their Time. Test scores were individualized, which confirmed the message to students that it was important to do their best. What was awesome is that scholars were eligible for every tier. So if they made it to tier three, they received all the prizes for tier one through tier three. I will give examples of how that looked. I will also list a few tips and scorecard samples.

So what's the message? No matter what task or activity is executed in your classroom, no child should ever feel left out. Just like when you plan for a math lesson, you scaffold to meet the needs of all scholars. When you plan for celebrations, find a way to count every child in. Everything in the classroom should be accessible to everyone. Some children don't try because they see limitations written into the prerequisites for success. I teach my children there are no prerequisites; I just need them to believe that anything—absolutely anything—is possible if they sow the seed of the absolute best within themselves.

A Little Compassion

Sometimes it's not that the scholar is being lazy, needs some intervention, or an additional service. Sometimes it's the structures in place, the pillars of our educational system, that are outdated. The US educational system is rolled out as a one-size-fits-all, which can limit students' ability to master the material in front of them. Not every child is meant to sit in front of a white board and listen to someone speaking. Some scholars need to be moving, interacting with manipulatives, and having a tangible experience during the lesson. But sadly, in most schools, that doesn't happen. Our educational construct put limits on scholars and forces them to conform to a specific way of processing information. It shouldn't be that way. So until the educational sector makes a decision to branch out and diversify its approach, as educators we have to. Our students deserve that and more.

Prizes & Strategies

Visualize	Script	Plan

~Testing Reward Tips~

Tip #1	Tip #2	Tip #3	Tip #3
-Have a conversation with students and explain to them how they may earn rewards. -The rewards table is usually set up and visual when students walk into class the morning of testing.	-Ask students what types of prizes they would like to earn. -Online stores are a great place to order prizes and party favors.	-Goodie bags may be as versatile or limited as you would like them to be. I bought party favors one year centered around certain themes and students were elated.	-The 'Top Secret' envelope is something you reveal at the official awards ceremony. Top Secret Prize Ideas: -Lunch Bunch with teacher (students choose menu) -Extra Recess -Movie Day with cinema snacks

Excellence is Written into Existence

~Example: Testing Rewards System~

- Testing Reward Criteria: Students may achieve rewards from multiple tiers. So if a student's achieves tier 3 status, that student receives the awards from all 3 tiers.

Reward Tier	Tier 1	Tier 2	Tier 3	Tier 4
Performance Criteria	Scholar Exhibits Growth *(even if its one point)*	Scholar Meets Winter Goal	Scholar Exceeds Winter Goal	Student Meets EOY Goal Early
Incentives	☐ Gold Crown ☐ 1 Pencil ☐ 1 Piece of Candy	☐ All Prizes from tier 1 ☐ Gold Medal ☐ Goodie Bag	☐ All Prizes from tiers 1 and 2 ☐ Cup Cake ☐ Homework Pass	☐ All Prizes from tiers 1, 2, and 3 ☐ Top Secret Envelope

Excellence is Written into Existence

~Testing Rewards System~

☐ Design and tailor you own rewards system for this coming school year.

Reward Tier	Tier 1	Tier 2	Tier 3	Tier 4
Performance Criteria				
Incentives				

Excellence is Written into Existence

∾ Score Card Tips∾

Discuss with students what their goals are for the upcoming test dates. These conversations should happen individually. It takes all of 3 minutes. When you print copies of scorecards, you may have students fill in their previous scores or, you may prefer to do it yourself. This happens before the official test date. These cards may also go home so parents may view their scholar's performance.

Excellence is Written into Existence

~Example: Single Subject Scorecard~

Student Name: Jane Doe.

❄ 3ʀᴅ GRADE WINTER 2021 ❄
MATH: SCORECARD

FALL SCORE	WINTER GOAL	WINTER GOAL	GROWTH STATUS
192	198	☐ Met	☑ I grew by <u>10</u> points!!!
	WINTER SCORE	☐ Not Met	
	202	☑ Exceeded	☐ I did not grow

Parent Signature: _____

Excellence is Written into Existence

~Blank Winter Scorecard~

Student Name: _____

🎖 WINTER SCORECARD 🎖

FALL SCORE	WINTER GOAL	WINTER GOAL	GROWTH STATUS
		☐ Met	☐ I grew by ____ points!!!
	WINTER SCORE	☐ Not Met	
		☐ Exceeded	☐ I did not grow

Parent Signature:

Excellence is Written into Existence

~Blank Spring Scorecard~

Student Name:

🏆 SPRING SCORECARD 🏆

WINTER SCORE	SPRING GOAL	WINTER GOAL	GROWTH STATUS
	SPRING SCORE	☐ Met ☐ Not Met ☐ Exceeded	☐ I grew by ____ points!!! ☐ I did not grow

Parent Signature:

Excellence is Written into Existence

~Example of Multi-Subject Scorecard~

Student Name: John Doe

❧ SPRING 2020 SCORECARD ❧

SUBJECT	WINTER SCORE	SPRING 2020 GOAL	SPRING 2020 PERFORMANCE	SPRING GOAL
Reading	198	205	Score: 207 I grew by **9** points!!!!	☐ Met ☐ Not Met ☑ Exceeded
Math	200	209	Score: 212 I grew by **12** points!!!!	☐ Met ☐ Not Met ☑ Exceeded

Excellence is Written into Existence

~Blank Multi-Subject Winter Scorecard~

Student Name: _____

❄ WINTER SCORECARD ❄

SUBJECT	FALL SCORE	WINTER GOAL	WINTER PERFORMANCE	WINTER GOAL
Reading			Score: I grew by ____ points!!!!	☐ Met ☐ Not Met ☐ Exceeded
Math			Score: I grew by ____ points!!!!	☐ Met ☐ Not Met ☐ Exceeded

Excellence is Written into Existence

~Blank Multi-Subject Spring Scorecard~

Student Name:

🌱 SPRING SCORECARD 🌱

SUBJECT	WINTER SCORE	SPRING GOAL	SPRING PERFORMANCE	SPRING GOAL
Reading			Score: I grew by ____ points!!!!	☐ Met ☐ Not Met ☐ Exceeded
Math			Score: I grew by ____ points!!!!	☐ Met ☐ Not Met ☐ Exceeded

Excellence is Written into Existence

∽Advocate & Cover∽

__It Wasn't Good Enough__

In everyday life, parents are a child's greatest advocates, loudest cheerleaders, and most important coverings. As an educator, you are your scholars' covering at school. One aspect of being a covering is being a protector. You are protecting your students' academic progress, self-confidence, and innocence. As an educator, it is your job to build an impenetrable fortress that protects the best interests of your students.

My message to my students is this: "I'm in your corner whether you are right or wrong. Good, bad, or indifferent, I have your backs." That, in no way, means my students escape the consequences of their poor choices. But it does mean that I'm there to support them in any way I can.

One year I was working for a particular organization, and at the beginning of the school year, all students were administered a reading test. Based on the data collected, grade level intervention groups were created.

I had a young man in my fourth-grade class that year who was reading at only a first-grade level. As a result, he was unable to access his schoolwork, and that frustration sometimes led him to act out. So, of course, I scaffolded and provided supplementary materials to meet him where he was, but intense intervention also was needed.

Fast forward: When we received the list of fourth graders who would receive reading intervention, my student's name was not on it, so I asked the administration why his name had been left off. I was told there wasn't enough room for him, which meant my scholar would have to wait for over three months to, possibly, receive intervention during the second round.

I thanked the administration for the information, and then I took matters into my own hands. I created a folder with samples of my student's work along with the scaffolds and supplementary materials I had been using. Then I found the reading interventionist, explained my student's situation, and showed her the materials I had gathered. She agreed almost immediately to pick him up five days a week when she picked up the reading intervention group for the first grade. We also made an extensive plan for him and created a digital data tracker that both of us could access. That was an arrangement that remained between us for the greater part of the school year. As my student's reading skills grew, the reading interventionist picked him up with the appropriate grade level group.

The unfortunate part of that story is that my student didn't make it onto the school's "official" intervention list until the end of April. The saving grace was that he had been receiving the intervention he needed all along, unbeknownst to the administration. By the time he was officially inserted into intervention, he had reached the beginning stages of a fourth-grade reading level.

My mindset as an educator the day I went to find the reading interventionist was that someone was going to help my child. It was like setting out a feast for his mind and then telling him he couldn't have access to it, and that was unacceptable. Even if the reading interventionist hadn't been able to help, I wanted to dialogue with her about what I could do because I was willing to use new materials and learn new strategies to assist him.

As an educator, you cannot take no for an answer. The moment you sense that your students need more help, take action and find a way to provide it—academically, socially, and emotionally. In your classroom, you scholars should want for absolutely nothing.

The Fine Print

One of the rules I have for my students is to respect every adult in the building—teachers, administrators, and office staff. No matter who it is, give the proper respect. But that rule also comes with fine print: "Sometimes adults make mistakes." Let me give an example.

It's a normal day, my students are in PE, and I'm doing some planning in my classroom. One of my students, let's call him Brandon, storms in, bangs his fist on the desk, and starts sobbing. I ask him what the problem is. He responds, "She called me big." So I ask him what happened. Brandon tells me students were playing sharks and minnows when he bumped into one of his classmates, and she fell. He helped her up, and they kept playing. But the PE teacher then yelled at Brandon, "You are too big to be bouncing around like that!"

Context: I was teaching third grade that year, and Brandon was the tallest student in my class. So after he told me the story, I thanked him for sharing and allowed him to do a math program until it was time for me to pick up my students. When I arrived, the first thing the teacher said to me was that Brandon had stormed out of class and never returned. I simply thanked the teacher for letting me know.

Fast forward: After school I went to the PE teacher and asked her if we could discuss the incident with Brandon. I explained my student's viewpoint, and I pointed out that her reference to his physical appearance was a trigger for him. I asked if she would be open to brainstorming how to get to know Brandon a little better. I understood that she worked with scores of children daily, so she may not know each of them as well as she might like. We had a productive conversation, and she said she understood how Brandon felt.

Some may say, "He still had no right to leave," or "You should have automatically been on the teacher's side." But I disagree. As educators, we never make reference to a child's physical appearance. Brandon, just like the rest of humanity, did not choose his physiological makeup. The comment the PE teacher made suggested there was imperfection in his appearance, and there was not. Bandon was exactly who he was supposed to be.

I also understand there are going to be enough conversations during Brandon's lifetime about how he has to conduct himself, so others don't feel threatened by the color of his skin or his stature. But school is one place he shouldn't have to concern himself with those things. His focus should be on succeeding academically and enjoying being a nine-year-old little boy.

I always tell my students, "If you are treated unfairly by any staff member, I want to hear everything you have to say. I want to hear your side. I just need you to wait until I pick you up from recess, music, lunch, or science." And I tell my students, "If you try and handle it, you can make the resolution more complicated, but that doesn't mean you are wrong." I support my colleagues, but I also recognize my students have feelings and concerns that should be addressed. When you are one educator in a room with thirty-five students, you may have responded to something in the moment that wasn't at all what it seemed. It happens, but there is always a remedy. After all, we're all human. That is the fine print.

Confidence in Your Craft

We all know the saying, "Teamwork makes the dream work." We also know the saying that it takes a village to raise a child. In the school building, that village consists of educators, office staff, the custodial staff, the cafeteria staff, and on and on. Children should feel like they can depend on at least one person to take an interest in them.

We have all seen the student who doesn't respond well to his primary teacher but, for some reason, responds to the office manager. We have seen that little girl who will scream at the top of her lungs until the lunch lady turns the corner and simply asks what she needs, and suddenly the world is a happy place. Maybe seven other people had already asked, but the lunch lady is her person at school.

As an educator, have enough confidence in your craft to know that, sometimes, a scholar's provision is going to come from outside your boundaries—academically, socially, or emotionally. It does not take away from your value in that child's life. It doesn't mean you're not a good teacher. But what is in the best interests of a student cannot be laced with ego or insecurity. You are on a team, and as team player you should want everybody to win. That includes teachers and students. I will share a few of my own experiences to give a picture of how you can implement this concept into your daily execution as an educator.

Scenario 1: *Confidence in Your Craft*

One year, for some reason, the boys in my class would show up without their hair being brushed. That happened at least twice a week. The beauty supply store sold hairbrushes for $2 apiece, so I bought some and wrote individual names on each brush with a permanent marker. Then I put the brushes into some cool little bags I picked up at the store. Then, on one Thursday afternoon, I kept my boys in the classroom during their enrichment period. We had a male staff member who many of the young men looked up to. He was one of only two male educators on staff that year. I arranged for him to stop by. He and my boys put their chairs in a circle, and I handed him the bin of brand-new hairbrushes and left the room. The boys and the male teacher then had a conversation, and during that conversation he showed them how to brush their hair. From my understanding, he also spoke with them about the importance of keeping up their general appearance. From that point on there was a drawer where my boys had access to their individual hair brush every morning. That same male educator would stop by at least twice a week to greet my boys and see who was using the techniques he had taught them.

Two things had happened. One, that event opened the door for my boys to build a rapport with a male staff member that, for some, was the only positive relationship they had with a male authority figure. Two, they knew someone had shown an interest in them.

I know some may say I could have told them how to brush their hair myself or shown them a step-by-step video online.

But no, I understood the power of a man having that conversation with them. The messenger matters, and that message was received differently from the male teacher than it would have been from me. And seeing how my boys' eyes lit up when the male teacher stopped by some mornings and said, "You guys look sharp today," or "I'm proud of you guys," did something for me as well.

Bringing the male teacher in didn't take away from who I was as their primary teacher. But my boys needed something I could not give them, a male voice taking a moment to breathe life into their identity as young men.

Scenario 2: Confidence in Your Craft

One year I was teaching one second grade class among multiple cohorts. We noticed a trend not only in their test scores but also in our daily classes. So a colleague and I who taught on the second-grade team got together and came up with a plan that would be implemented after the holiday season for the remainder of the school year.

Every day we had eighty minutes for small group instruction in reading, so I would send my students who needed heavy scaffolding to her classroom, and she would send the kids who were performing on or above grade level to me. The amount of growth we saw over the next two months was astounding. That eighty-minute block was so tailored to where they were as a collective that the students who needed heavy scaffolding didn't feel rushed to comprehend, and the others were no longer sitting idly by because they weren't being challenged. The students' confidence shot through the roof because they weren't so nervous about answering questions. It was two-and-a-half months down the line before the administration realized what was going on.

Why am I sharing this? It's because I want you to see this wasn't about competition. As educators, my colleague and I both had skill sets that were useful, but those skill sets were most productive when we worked as a team. It does no good when one team member's class soars in growth and test scores while another teacher's class flounders. When that does happen, it's the children who are losing. My colleague understood certain aspects of reading when it came to moving children that were below grade level that, at the time,

I did not. There was no need to feel shame. We were both open and wanted our children to succeed by any means necessary, and we got it done.

As an educator, don't be afraid to ask questions. No one person has all the answers. The field of education is like medicine in that it's ever evolving with new practices and improved strategies being discovered almost every day. Empower your colleagues. Not everyone is going to be receptive, and not everyone is going to want to share. But remember this: remain humble and remain teachable. Whether you are an administrator or primary teacher, the moment you become unteachable is the day you stagnate. Don't dim the light of those around you by trying to prove your worth. Be confident, and know that what you bring to the school every day is unique and divinely fashioned because there is only one you.

Beyond Physical Safety

Conflict resolution directly ties to the atmosphere in the classroom, and that atmosphere is determined by the teacher. In recent years, schools have emphasized mental health as well as academics. As the conversation surrounding mental health has become louder, as it should—there is no shame in taking care of yourself—we should be teaching our youth to do the same.

We are discussing this because classrooms all over this nation are generally safe spaces physically but not necessarily socially or emotionally. There are schools all over this nation that push for physical safety but ignore the social and emotional aspects.

Physical safety is not enough. During distance learning there were some children who actually found peace of mind because they weren't at school where they were regularly being bullied or ostracized. We all know students do what we call "playing the dozens" where they trade insults to see whose words can cut the deepest.

But as an educator, that sort of conduct cannot be allowed, ever. Most physical altercations start after verbal jabs have been thrown. I am not ashamed to say there are consequences in my classroom if I find a student insulted someone or was engaged in bullying of any kind. No parent should have to worry if their child is going to spend the majority of the school day being made to feel like an outcast.

No child should dread coming to school because they feel alone.

Most classrooms that have poor classroom management have no expectation of how students should treat each other. I tell my students, "You don't have to be friends, but you will respect each other at all times. You will refer to each other on a first-name basis only." Also, I heavily incentivize acts of kindness.

My students know they earn extra rewards points when they help a classmate who is struggling on a math problem. My boys know Ms. Huff is probably going to say, "Go to the treasure chest" because they held the door for a young lady.

Bullying of any kind should be nipped in the bud. We all have had coworkers who see their children, especially the younger ones, engaging in such conduct, yet the teachers act like they see nothing. Ignoring such behavior leads to a toxic and emotionally unsafe environment for the children. Sometimes students are not used to being held to a higher standard in how they relate to others, but that is no excuse. Teach them a new and better way.

✒Fun and Accountability✒

Lesson Learned

As educators we should personalize incentives in our classroom, whether that is rewards at the end of the week or the month. One thing I teach my students is that privileges must be earned and maintained, and we go over the difference between a privilege and a right.

I teach my children the power of preservation, so they don't develop a sense of entitlement. Should educators be allowed to take privileges and grant them based upon student behavior? In short, yes. I know some schools prefer teachers not take recess away under any circumstances. In the last few years, I have heard of schools restricting any type of student accountability system.

Most of us didn't grow up that way. Actions had two outcomes—reward or consequence. A reward could have been earning a gift card. A consequence could have been taking ten minutes off your recess, or maybe you didn't get to go on a field trip outside of school. But now some schools are telling teachers what they can't do without giving them strategies to maintain a system of accountability in their classrooms.

My students are rewarded handsomely for their daily performances. What do incentives in my classroom look like? There are video games they can play in class, and my scholars are allowed to bring toys from home that are cleared by parents. Students also can earn free time, and I keep a refrigerator in my room that along with a large snack bin. I also have a treasure chest filled with toys, among other things.

Some may say that's a lot, but it really isn't. My students are sometimes with me from 7:45 in the morning until 4:15 in the afternoon, so the classroom should feel like home. If you work hard, you also should play hard, as the saying goes.

The following is an example of when I took my students' privileges due to poor decision- making.

One day my students were dropped off by a staff member at music class, which took place in the auditorium. There was a substitute that day, and we all know how that can go. So the moment the staff member who transitioned them walked away, my students decided to start chasing each other around the auditorium, up and down the aisles, hopping over the chairs, just having a grand old time. The substitute had to get assistance, and the principal had to intervene. At the end of the class, I walked in to pick up my students, and the principal informed me of what had taken place. As the principal was speaking, my students were off to the side staring at the floor, avoiding all eye contact with me. As you know, that meant they felt guilty and were coming up with ways to defend their actions.

When we returned to the classroom, we had a brief conversation. You could hear a pin drop. My students knew my rule: respect every adult in the building. And they knew that consequences would follow after I received the report of their lack of respect. We all knew they wouldn't have dared to pull something like that had the regular music teacher been present. But it shouldn't have mattered if the regular teacher was there or not. There was an adult present who had given them a directive.

The conversation ended with this statement from me, which hit them like a ton of bricks: "No video games, no toys, no special snacks, no TV for the next three days." You would have thought I had taken their recess away for a month with the way they responded. But I didn't have to touch recess.

Some may say I was harsh, but I prefer they learn at the age of nine or ten that there are consequences for your actions. They needed to be reminded that the freedom to play a video game or play with toys from home was a privilege that needed to be earned. I needed them to handle going to enrichment class respectfully and to conduct themselves like scholars while there. It is safe to say they didn't make that mistake again for the remainder of the school year.

Then on Some Days

As hard as I push my students on their academics and as high as my expectations are for them, there are days we come to class and do absolutely nothing. I will stand in front of the class on those mornings and ask, "What do you all want to do today?" Hands shoot up, and the responses vary: play video games, play with our toys, go outside, watch TV, make an art project. Yes, some of my students even ask to sleep for an hour or two. Don't judge; it's their time.

Here's the thing: days like that usually come after results have been proven. So if we take state testing and 75 percent of the class scores in the ninetieth percentile, we take a day for ourselves. If we take interims and they're outperforming not only their peers within the district but the city as a whole, you better believe we're going to celebrate and take some time for ourselves. I try to incorporate free time outside of recess weekly anyway, but it's never the whole day. So having the entire day for my students to do what they want is a major treat for them.

In my experience that strategy usually motivates students to push that much harder. It gives them drive when lessons resume the day after a breather. Have administrators walked into my classroom during some of those moments? Yes, but they don't fight the vibe.

Speaking from a transparent place, I've had principals tell me they can't figure it out. Administrators have made statements like, "Your students have a lot of freedom or flexibility, but they are well behaved" (disclaimer: *most of the time*). They can't figure out how students are thriving academically when I allow them to move and maneuver in ways other educators would see as chaotic.

The system works because there is balance. Everything from my expectations, to the way I speak to them, from the non-negotiables to the freedoms they are given, is implemented with a purpose. Free choice and free thinking allow the mind to operate on a higher plain. As an educator, you take days off when you need a mental break. Students sometimes need the opportunity to do the same thing.

~Affirm~

Affirm: *"1. To declare positively; assert to be true. 2. To declare support for or belief in."*[i]

Another practice we should follow as educators is affirming our students every day by reminding them of their endless capabilities and how amazing they are. Your words as an authority figure have power. Your words can be what boosts students' confidence, or they can be students' memories ten years later of someone telling them they weren't going amount to anything.

Children can sense when you genuinely have taken an interest in them and their success. One year I was working with a fourth-grade class, and every single day I would tell them, "There is nobody better than you." We also had a call and response. I would shout, "Is there anybody better than you?" My students would shout back, "No!" And the more they did it, the more they believed it, and then it started to manifest itself beyond academics.

When there were other fourth-grade classes around, my students took pride in being the example of how to conduct themselves. Anytime there was a competition, be it sports, academics, or whatever, they won. Enrichment teachers would stop by the classroom impromptu just to tell me how proud they were of our class. When my students' test scores came out, my students not only received recognition within the school but in the city. Their success, accolades, and other recognition wasn't because they always had everything together. But they believed. Your mindset helps determine how you perform; that's just human nature.

There is nobody better than you. Was that a strong statement to make? Maybe. Did I mean it? Yes, I did. But when the school year started, our class was not an exact reflection of that statement. Yet every time we did that call and response, I was challenging them to rise to the occasion. The greatest gains students made that school year were not in their test scores or in school competitions but in their character. Those students left my classroom that June operating at a higher frequency than when they entered. The world around them changed for the better, but first, we had to change the world they experienced within themselves.

Scaffold How You Affirm

Another part of this strategy is teaching students how to affirm themselves. That works differently with each grade level. When I taught second grade, every day in morning meeting one child would stand and lead the class in their affirmations. It was always fresh because every child led the affirmations with their own style, flair, and personality. If we didn't do the affirmations, students wanted to know why.

I hold a firm belief that all scholars are nothing short of a fulfilled purpose and destiny in the making. But I need them to know that for themselves. There are well over one hundred days of school, so my students had the opportunity to declare those things to themselves many times. Whether its tomorrow and ten years from now. I believe the affirmative words my scholars spoke about themselves over and over again will come to pass. I know some may wonder if that's all that's necessary, and the answer is yes. Not every scholar who enters your classroom has the highest self-esteem or would even know how to begin to see the world differently. That's why, as an educator, it's your job to believe for them until they can believe for themselves.

∽Examples of Affirmations∽

Ms. Huff's Second Graders' Daily Affirmations

Today is a new day, and it will be great.
I am smart.
I am amazing.
I can do anything.
I am powerful beyond measure.
I believe in my future. My dreams will come true.
I am going to college; I will change the world.
I respect myself and others.
My hands are for excellence.
My minds is for mastery.
I won, I conquered because I believed.

Grade Level Idea:

When I moved to fourth grade, I tweaked the practice a little. At the beginning of each month, I gave students a note card. The students wrote one affirmation for themselves for the month. Some students taped it on top of their desks, and some taped it inside. But we took thirty seconds every morning so students could say their personal affirmation to themselves. If you decide to use this practice, be creative, and don't forget to include your scholars in the planning process.

Affirm

| Visualize | Script | Plan |

Excellence is Written into Existence

~Affirm with Words~

☐ List two goals in each category where you would like to see student growth.

Academics	In their Character	Social & Emotional Skills
1.	1.	1.
2.	2.	2.

☐ What quotes or affirmations will you utilize daily to encourage student growth in those areas?

Academics	Character	Social Emotional Skills

Excellence is Written into Existence

~Script and Plan~

☐ Create a list of affirmations students can recite as a class daily. This is a great way to close out morning meeting. These affirmations should promote the classroom culture you desire to build as an educator. Use an anchor chart to create a visual for students.

1. _____
2. _____
3. _____
4. _____
5. _____
6. _____
7. _____

Excellence is Written into Existence

~Affirming Beyond the Classroom~

- [ ] What strategies will you use to teach scholars to affirm themselves? Map out tools they can use outside the school building.

Excellence is Written into Existence

Create a Dialogue

Ask the Question

One of the powerful questions you can ask parents is this: what is your vision for your child? It's a question that opens a dialogue. It welcomes parents into their child's academic journey. The question also gives parents a voice in their scholar's daily experience in your classroom. The moment you open that dialogue, you are laying the groundwork to build a sense of community. Ask parents about their scholar's strengths and areas that need growth. Ask about their scholar's likes, dislikes, and hobbies.

The response to that question also will give you a glimpse into how parents view their scholars. In a perfect world, all parents would think the best of their scholars and see them as pioneers of change and greatness, but that's not always the case. When I listen or read a parent's response, it gives me context about a scholar's disposition. Do the students believe in themselves? Do they know they are worthy of every good opportunity that comes their way? Do they have a vision for their future?

We've all encountered parents who have nothing positive to say about their scholars, which is unfortunate. But that is included in the job description for us as educators. Filling in the gaps is a layered task. Every scholar has more great qualities than areas of growth. It's the job of parents and educators to help scholars mature in those areas.

A parent's response is also a great tool to start a portfolio for a scholar. Its gives you a blueprint of what a parent is looking for. For example, if parents say their six-year-old needs to work on sharing, then I know that when I see growth in that area, mom and dad are going to be elated to hear the great news. Also, when it comes to academics, parents may share that a child struggles in reading. That gives you, as an educator, focal points to emphasize during a parent-teacher conference. Ask parents the question. When it comes to their child, what is their vision?

Open Door Policy

In some corporate, political, and private sector settings there is what is called an open-door policy. Employees are allowed to share their ideas, ask questions, or voice concerns. In a perfect world they could do so without fear of retaliation. The classroom should run the same way.

Students have ideas, suggestions, and their own way of processing things, and they want to share them, even though you may not be able to implement their ideas immediately, if at all. You can still show that you value what they have to say simply by listening. That builds rapport.

But I do tell my students not to complain about what they don't have in the classroom if they haven't asked for it. One day I had some chicken wings sitting on my desk, and a student let's call him, John asked if he could have one. I said, "Yes." John returned to his seat, loudly smacking his lips and savoring every bite. John's partner stared at him and then at me before he raised his hand and asked, "Ms. Huff, how did he get to have a wing?" My response was, "He asked."

I know some may say, sure, you let your students ask for that. But I don't treat my students just as students; I treat them as if they were my own children. And most parents will tell you that, usually, you can't have anything to yourself.

Another time we were in class, and the students were working on a problem set. A student who had gone to the restroom returned, and a few students had special erasers they loved to use during math. They called them "jelly erasers" because they were clear. When the returning student sat down, I noticed he wasn't writing. I walked over and asked if he needed help. "I didn't get a jelly eraser," he said. My response was, "Did you ask for one?" He said no. I jokingly gasped in shock, and he smiled before he said, "Could I have one?" I said yes.

There's nothing my students can't ask me for, although my answer will sometimes be no.

Open communication is essential in the classroom because there may come a day when the students need to share something more serious. But if being able to talk to their primary teacher seems foreign to them, that creates a barrier, even when it comes to asking for things or privileges. I'd prefer to know that students have a need or want than for them to remain silent. Again, sometimes the answer will be no, but at least they will have the confidence to ask.

Open Door Policy

Visualize	Script	Plan

~Example: Avenues to Communicate~

☐ This chart shows examples of various ways students may communicate with teachers.

Note Card Parking Lot
(Posted in Classroom)

- A poster that is on public display in the classroom
- Students may leave ideas for field trips
- Students may also leave ideas for "Fun Friday'

Concern Box
(Students peers do not read these messages)

- Students may share anonymously if they are having trouble with peers
- Students may also share anonymously if they need to review a lesson from the day before. Sometimes students are afraid to ask for help publicly.

Digital Platform
(those approved and provided by the school)

- Students may ask questions pertaining to homework
- Students may also view what homework was assigned, if they may have been absent that day or forgot to write it down.

Excellence is Written into Existence

Avenues to Communicate

☐ List 3 ways students may communicate their ideas, suggestions, and thoughts with you. Remember it's their classroom too, and they should feel included in its day-to-day operation. Explain to students these modes of communication are available.

_____
- Purpose:
- Purpose:

_____
- Purpose:
- Purpose:

_____
- Purpose:
- Purpose:

Excellence is Written into Existence

Weekly Communication Helps

We live in a technology age. We communicate with people we've never met, which can make things much easier for educators. One practice that is foolproof is a weekly newsletter to parents. Communication is everything. Why? Because parents can't always make it to the school building. You would be surprised how invested parents become when the invitation to share information is extended. They start looking forward to updates from their child's teacher. So what does a typical newsletter look like? Individual teachers have their own flair, but I will share some of my basics.

At the top there is always a banner or letterhead identifying the class, grade level, subject, or school. Below that you could insert classroom pictures or art. Then comes the homework chart. When the newsletter goes out on Sunday evenings, it lists all homework assignments students are responsible for that week. That is a lifesaver because parents may not know if a scholar has homework or not. A newsletter also covers you during report card week because you have a paper trail of the information you shared with families.

Next comes a brief greeting in which you share some class highlights and other important information. If there is a quiz or test coming up, I usually list what is going to be covered. Parents appreciate that because it creates an avenue to help their students prepare. Then you want to have a small column for important dates for events such as school closings, exam dates, field trips, and school plays and concerts.

Finally, you always want to leave your contact information. How much you share is up to your discretion. Some educators share an email and reminder that they can be reached through a digital platform. Some educators share their cell phone information. Do what makes you comfortable.

A newsletter can be tailored to your class, or your grade level may want to create one as a cohort. There are so many platforms now to share information, so you should tailor your newsletter to your organization's blueprint.

The last item is what I call a double share. The newsletter is posted to the schools' digital platform of choice, for all families. But in my experience, sometimes parents do not consistently use the platform, so I create an email list for my classroom. I send it so parents receive individualized emails, just in case. Students are much more accountable when their parents have been previewed to their academic expectations.

Leadership

One of the most important aspects of being a leader is being present. There is no use in being the leader of your classroom if you never come to work. Even a Fortune 500 CEO has to show up. It makes a huge difference when leaders can see for themselves what is going well and what needs improvement.

This is a message to CEOs, founders, and COOs of schools all over this nation: your presence, genuine interest, and voice never reach a point where they are no longer needed. Some CEOs need to escape their offices and make an effort that goes beyond showing up at the corporate headquarters every day. Your staff may have seen you once this school year, and most of them have never heard you ask, "How are things going?" That question holds so much weight. Some of your staff have no idea what you even look like.

There are organizations that have seventeen people between the top leader and the educators on the front lines. As a CEO, your presence demands accountability from everybody. There are principals who need that push. Then they would understand that they can't handle staff any way they wish because the CEO can walk in at any moment. Those in leadership would be more cognizant of their management styles if they understood the CEO was going to ask their staff directly and in confidence, "How are you doing?"

But some CEOs and founders of educational institutions are literally nowhere to be found. For some of you who can't figure out why your turnover rate is so high or why your staff is so miserable, maybe it's time you stop sending liaisons to speak to staff and have a conversation with them yourself. That goes for superintendents as well.

I know some may say they have confidence in those they have hired to lead their various campuses, but as a CEO you can't just have confidence in the credentials of those you have put in leadership positions. You also need confidence in their character. If a person doesn't have the character for the position they hold, it deems the position powerless. A leader may have five degrees but not know how to communicate effectively. Some of your leaders have run top educators out the door by using intimidation, passive aggression, and other bullying tactics. But guess what, CEO? That falls on you. You're the face of the organization and the ultimate leader.

Principles, vice principals, and school administrators should know that being in leadership is not about barking orders; it's about having a mindset to serve. If you're in charge, one of your main focuses should be on how you can make life easier for your staff. Ask yourself, "What can I do to make sure the day runs a little bit smoother for my staff? Is there anything I can take on today that would remove some of the weight from their shoulders?"

This following is a true story. There was a CEO of a charter school I worked for who would show up at the building, put her things in the principal's office and, for the two hours she was there she would be on the move. She would walk into classrooms and speak to teachers and students. She asked simple questions like, "Do have any copies you need to make?" That CEO wouldn't watch the class; she would go make the copies for the teacher herself, right then and there. If she ran into a teacher transitioning students to lunch or recess, she would ask the teacher where they were headed. She would then say to the teacher, "I can take them. There is fresh coffee and donuts in the lounge. Please help yourself." That CEO always brought something to show gratitude to teachers. If you were a visitor in the building, you would have thought she was a primary teacher by the way she carried herself. She had a mindset to serve. That CEO wasn't there daily or even weekly, but she would visit each campus at least once a month. The students, teachers, and parents knew who she was personally.

Your organization should never be so large that you fall out of touch, because the wellbeing of students hangs in the balance. If students' wellbeing is limited to or defined by an organization's name being on the top of the list for testing scores, it's time to review the original mission. The investment an organization makes in its staff has a direct effect on the investment teachers make in their students.

CEOs and administrators are supposed to be to their staff what they expect their staff to be to their students. Staff are required to cultivate a learning environment that boasts academic gains as well as social, emotional, and mental wellbeing. Make the same effort to ensure your organization is a great place to work. Set the standard not only for academic success but for what a peaceful organization with great pay and work-life balance looks like. It's never too late for change.

~It Is Written~

A New Name

One particular day I was off campus, and my phone kept going off. When I finally answered, it was a coworker. The first thing she said was, "Ms. Huff, your children are so high maintenance." Of course, I wanted to know what she meant. My coworker informed me that the substitute teacher had brought my children in from recess and taken them to the water fountain. My students then informed the substitute they didn't drink from water fountains, and they refused to do so.

My students were telling the truth. I kept a refrigerator in my room that held water bottles and juice boxes for my kids to have whenever they liked. Why am I telling this story? Every school year, staff made comments to me like, "Your children are spoiled, entitled, or bougie." My response was always, "Thank you."

Here is the kicker: every year I have taught in the classroom I have worked with what society would deem "at risk or underprivileged youth." Let's stop there for a second because, at the start of every school year, those labels seem to be the focus and the children's permanent identity. Schools take plenty of time to prepare for the negative. For example, we sit through professional development to deal with student trauma. But do we give the same attention to teaching our students about existing in a state of happiness within themselves? After all, many have to return to the exact environment that manifested the trauma in the first place.

I would never stand in front of my students and tell them they are underprivileged or at risk or keep reminding them they live in poverty. So, I don't identify students with those labels when they aren't in the room.

But I will continue to instill in my students their divine right to tap into their privilege that manifests excellence. Why? Because there is a code of privilege that is written into their DNA; it just has to be activated.

What I want my students to know is that their privilege is not limited to football or basketball or baseball. My students' privilege is so powerful that it radiates throughout the universe. It is the reason certain programs are snatched from certain schools so children from a particular race or background never have the opportunity to tap into their divine potential.

May we deal with the obvious? If students with divine gifting are offered too many resources, there is an excellent chance they may surpass their counterparts who were given a head start. Some of the powers that be will tell you in so many words that they won't have that. For them, success needs to have a certain face or pedigree. It's the reason some children in certain school districts are given just enough. But in spite of that, some of those children who have been boxed in keep rising to the occasion.

What we don't teach our children is that, even from birth, destiny is always whispering their name through life experience, a natural talent, or genuine interest in a subject they desperately want to explore.

There is a little boy who is naturally gifted in the flute, but where does he have the opportunity to tap into and grow that divine gift? There is a little boy who loves to take things apart to see what's inside and put them back together. Some would call him destructive, but he only needs a robotics club to exercise his skills. Something is calling out to him, even at the age of five.

There is a little girl who is genuinely interested in physics, but her school doesn't even teach science. All the science labs were removed from her school district. There is a little girl who is curious about the medical field. She has a desire to cure cancer, even at the age of eight, because someone close to her is suffering. And there is that one student we all have had who can effortlessly alter the classroom atmosphere—negative or positive—that student is a leader.

So why did I tell the story about the water fountain? Because at the beginning of the school year, society, the administration, and even some teachers kept labeling students as "at-risk." It doesn't mean they meant it in a degrading way, but by the middle of the school year those same students they kept referring to as "at-risk" were being called by a new name. I'd prefer you say my kids are bougie than to keep saying they are "at risk." Words have power ...

While we're on the subject of at-risk youth, that label tells a much deeper truth. There are millions of youths who are at-risk, and not because of their zip code or socioeconomic status. They are at-risk of never finding out or tapping into who they truly are. Some students exist in a system that identifies them as at-risk but that also builds barriers to keep them that way.

The risk of a lost or dormant identity should be eliminated every morning when students hit the threshold of the school building. A big piece to that puzzle is for every child in the nation to be extended the same first-class education, resources, and opportunities.

I inform my students that excellence in my classroom is not optional. The reason is, as an educator, I understand their excellence is already written.

Educator's Journal

Visualize	Script	Plan

✏️ Write Your Vision ✏️

_____
_____
_____
_____
_____
_____
_____
_____
_____
_____
_____
_____
_____
_____
_____
_____

Excellence is Written into Existence

Write Your Vision

Excellence is Written into Existence

Write Your Vision

Excellence is Written into Existence

Write Your Vision

Excellence is Written into Existence

Write Your Vision

Excellence is Written into Existence

Write Your Vision

Excellence is Written into Existence

Write Your Vision

_____
_____
_____
_____
_____
_____
_____
_____
_____
_____
_____
_____
_____
_____
_____
_____
_____
_____
_____
_____
_____
_____
_____

Excellence is Written into Existence

Information

Imagine exceeding the contents of this book. You can change the social and operational structure of your school, organization, or classroom. Dramatically improve the educational services offered to students, and the work environment employees experience daily.

Are you interested in…

- ❏ Math Instructional Coaching (virtual or in-person)
- ❏ Data Analysis Strategies
- ❏ Classroom Culture Strategies
- ❏ Reshaping Organizational Constructs
- ❏ Consulting

To invite Mya to speak at your next professional development or event. Get in touch by emailing info.MyaHuff@gmail.com.

Excellence is Written into Existence

Notes

[i] The American Heritage Desk Dictionary, Fifth Edition (Boston: Houghton Mifflin Harcourt, 2013), "Affirm"

www.ingramcontent.com/pod-product-compliance
Lightning Source LLC
Chambersburg PA
CBHW050435010526
44118CB00013B/1540